Words from
My Window

Words from My Window

A JOURNAL

RUSKIN BOND

Illustrations by

DAN WILLIAMS

PENGUIN BOOKS

An imprint of Penguin Random House

PENGUIN BOOKS

USA | Canada | UK | Ireland | Australia
New Zealand | India | South Africa | China | Singapore

Penguin Books is part of the Penguin Random House group of companies
whose addresses can be found at global.penguinrandomhouse.com

Published by Penguin Random House India Pvt. Ltd.
4th Floor, Capital Tower 1, MG Road,
Gurugram 122 002, Haryana, India

First published in Penguin Books by Penguin Random House India 2019

10 9 8 7 6 5

ISBN 9780670092239

Typeset in EB Garamond

Printed at Replika Press Pvt. Ltd., India

www.penguin.co.in

TO MY READERS

In a way, this journal is an ode to my window,
or rather, to all the windows I have possessed
throughout my life; for without a window I doubt if
I would have been half the writer that I am today.

I need a window to look at the world without; for only then
can I look at the world within. A room without a window
is rather like a prison cell, and the soul is inclined to shrivel
up in a confined space. Shade is welcome only when there is
a strong sun. Great works may have been written in prison
cells, but for most of us a room with a window is preferable
to staring at four dark walls. And you don't have to be a poet
to appreciate the visible presence of the sky, clouds, rain,
sunshine, and the caress of a cool breeze.

I have lived most of my life in small rooms, but they have
almost always had windows opening out onto a greater
world. In those early days, there was my 'room on the roof'

which gave me my first novel. Later, in London and Dehradun and New Delhi there were windows which gave me views of busy streets, and those were fine, because streets full of people are streets full of stories. And when I came to live in the hills, there was at first Maplewood, with its windows opening onto a small forest of oak and maple trees, and sometimes I received visitors from the forest—birds, beetles, even a tiny bat!—and then I came up the mountain to my room in Landour, and for thirty years I have sat at this desk before my window, writing stories, poems, and memoirs like this one, and never once have I felt bored or alone in this world, for something is always happening outside. Today, there are a couple of pigeons on the windowsill, one cooing, the other silent. Other sounds, car horns, children calling to each other as they return from school, a boy selling candyfloss, several crows chasing a hawk! Never a dull moment. And the magic mountain looks on, absorbing everything.

Dan Williams spent several hours at my window and days on the hillside, busy with his sketch pad. His lovely watercolours adorn this journal and capture the essence of my life up here. This book is as much his as it is mine.

Ruskin Bond
15 May 2019

I have had a happy and fulfilling life and have given enjoyment to a few readers, young and old.

I'm a person without many regrets.

So here I am, delving into the past like Monsieur Poirot,

not to solve a mystery, but to try to understand some of the events that have helped define the sort of person I have become. Some of it, naturally, is in the genes; but much of it is in the environment, in the circumstances in which we grow up, in the people who come into our lives, even in the air we breathe.

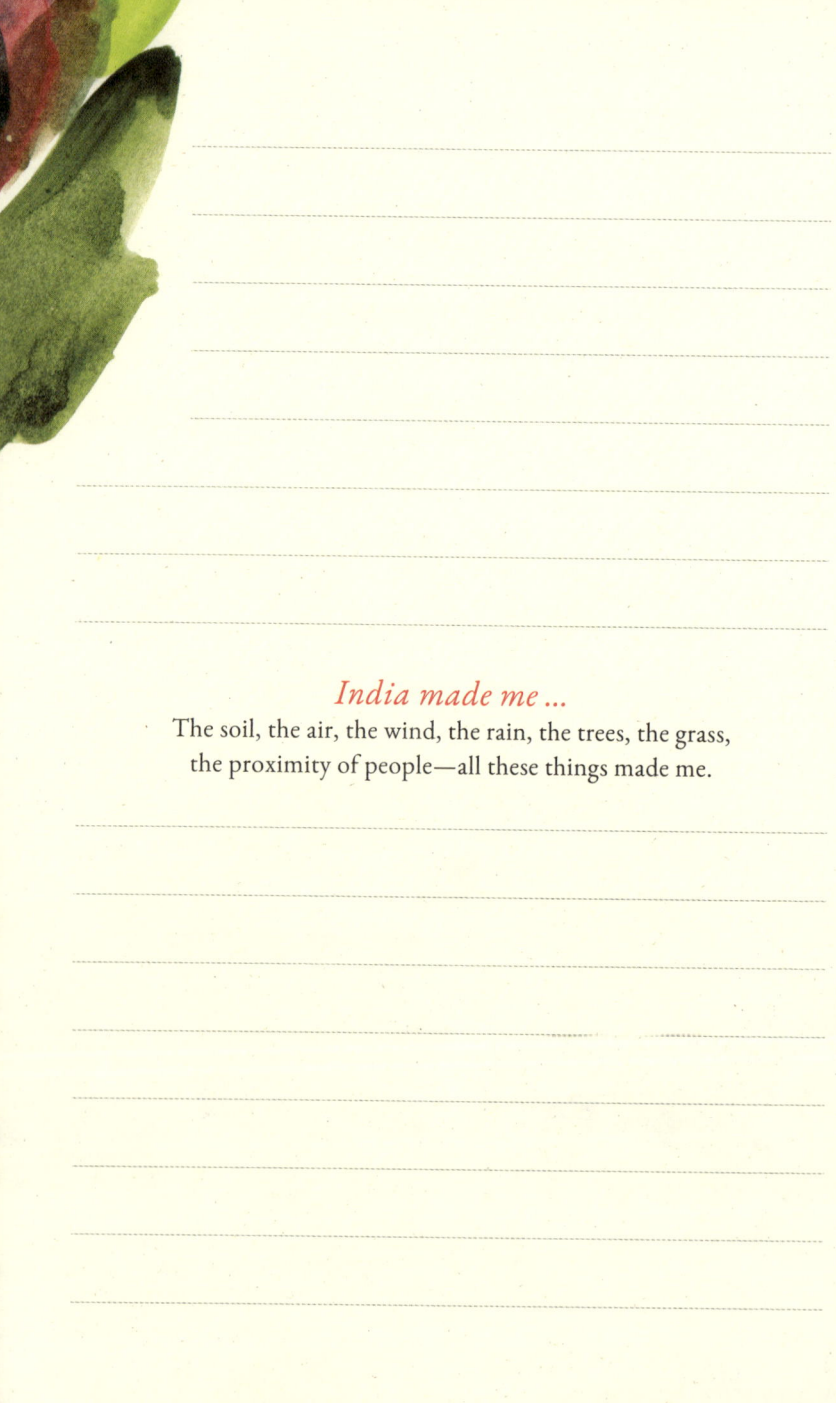

India made me ...
The soil, the air, the wind, the rain, the trees, the grass,
the proximity of people—all these things made me.

This ... is a remembrance of times past, an attempt to resurrect a person or a period or an episode, a reflection on the unpredictability of life.

Some paths lead nowhere; others lead to a spring of pure water. Take any path and hope for the best. At least it will lead you out of the shadows.

*Dormitory life seems to suit some
people but I've always wanted my
own space, my own private room,
even if it's a small one.*

I demanded (and got) a room of my
own, albeit a tiny one ...

It was a model of a Spitfire, a fighter plane, the plane that had defended London during the German Blitz.

It had been given to my father, then serving in the RAF. He had died earlier that year in Calcutta ...

That box of earthly treasures was kept under my bed, and no one was allowed to touch it ...

I loved watering the flowers. I watered
them, I would address them by name,
'Petunias, good morning!'

*'Snapdragons, how are you
today?' 'Zinnias, you look thirsty!'
'Yellow rose, you look lovely
today!' 'Sweet peas, enjoy a
shower this morning!'*

*History only tells us about the great ones
who left their footprints on the sands of time.*

Dhuki spent most of his life growing sweet peas
and petunias for an old lady. ... That's the kind of
life I try to celebrate!

I think it was Brian ... who discovered the tunnel.
... This excited us. To find a secret passage that
would take us out of the school boundary ...

It hadn't taken us anywhere, really, but to be outside the
school, instead of inside, made a lot of difference to us from
a psychological viewpoint. ... but we had broken bounds,
and that made us feel special. Now I am over seventy years
distant from our little tunnel in my boarding school; but
all my life I have been on the lookout for tunnels. ... That
passage to England was a tunnel of sorts.

_____

_____

_____

_____

_____

*1946 . . . One of my
best years in school.*

I played hockey and football for the school's junior team, discovered
Dickens, and wrote my first 'novel', which was confiscated by my
Housemaster, never to be seen again! In the same year my friends
and I tunnelled our way out of the school grounds.

If only the world had no boundaries and we could move about
without hindrance, without having to produce passports
and documents everywhere (even within one's own country),
it really would be
'a great wide beautiful wonderful world',
as a poet proclaimed ...

It took me away from a prison of my own making.

And in Jersey, when I was unhappy, I walked out of St Helier, its little port, and along the bays and beaches for mile after mile ... And I discovered London by walking all over the city ...

My window opens to the elements
—to the night air, to the day breeze,
to moonlight, to mist or sunshine,
to birds and insects, to the rhythm
of the seasons.

Little clouds enter my window. I let them in.
They are soft, caressing. They come in at the
window and slip out from the front door,
silent and discreet.

*There is still space in
front of my window.*

In fact, there is nothing between
me and Pari Tibba, the hill across the valley
... Pari Tibba, 'Hill of the Fairies', is directly
opposite us. If I could fly I'd be there in a
few minutes ...

I have always liked Christina Rossetti's poems,
especially the one that goes:

HURT NO LIVING THING;

LADYBIRD, NOR BUTTERFLY,

NOR MOTH WITH DUSTY WING,

NOR CRICKET CHIRPING CHEERILY,

NOR GRASSHOPPER SO LIGHT OF LEAP,

NOR DANCING GNAT, NOR BEETLE FAT,

NOR HARMLESS WORMS THAT CREEP.

*My first real writing room
was that tiny room on the roof,
a barsati on top of a rambling
old building in Dehradun,*

which had once been the Gresham
Hotel and later the Station Canteen
and was now occupied by various
tenants, among them my mother and
stepfather and my three small brothers
and sister.

There was an old Remington typewriter in my stepfather's automobile showroom,

and nobody seemed to be using it, so I brought it home, or rather carried it up to the barsati, which was at my disposal.

*I felt it was important for a writer
to keep a journal*

—and I had already read Somerset Maugham's
A Writer's Notebook, Sterne's *A Sentimental Journey*,
and the diaries of Samuel Pepys, so I knew the
importance of a journal or diary from a literary point
of view, but I also wanted to keep one in order to
preserve the memory of my friends.

A ship took me to England and the Channel Island.

And there, on the island of Jersey, at my aunt's house.

'1964 ... a little group about to set out on a picnic—Dick and Hetty Prim and their little girl Sunita (on the pony), Kamal, myself and Surekha (who was to become an actress)— and we must have had a couple of tiffin carriers with us too, because we carried our own food, there being no dhabas to greet us when we arrived at our destination. And where was our destination that day?

We were probably headed for the municipal garden (still called 'Company Bagh'), which would have been a 3-mile walk.'

I guess I was never really a ladies' man.

I was too immersed in my writing to bother much
with my clothes or appearance. Two pairs of trousers
and three shirts were the limit of my wardrobe ...

I wasn't the academic type, just a bookish boy and something of a dreamer.

I had already written a few stories, and although most of them had been rejected by magazine publishers, I was convinced that I had it in me to be a successful writer. And you had to go to London to be one!

The train rumbled and rocked
through the deserts of Rajasthan,

the forests of central India, the fertile plains
of Gujarat. We stopped at Baroda in the middle
of the night.

It was hot in the carriage ... A shadow fell against Lily's window, a hand slipped in, groped beneath her pillow and emerged with her purse tight within its grasp.

I gave a shout and leapt for the window; but the hand had disappeared, and bare feet took the thief—a skinny little fellow—speeding down the platform until he had disappeared into the darkness.

*We had two days in Bombay
before the ship sailed.
Mrs Shukla and Lily sped
off in a taxi, heading
for the Grand Hotel.*

I could not afford such a posh
destination. I got into a tonga, a
pony cart, with my two suitcases
and a mora—a mora being a small
wicker-cane stool, very light and
easy to carry about. What was I
doing with a mora, as I awaited my
passage to England? Well, my aunt
in Jersey wanted one.

I was finally deposited outside a
seedy little hotel on Lamington Road ...
There was no window, not even a skylight. ...

My only companion was a lizard, a gecko, who spent
all his time on the walls or ceiling, waiting patiently for
a careless fly or mosquito to come his way ...

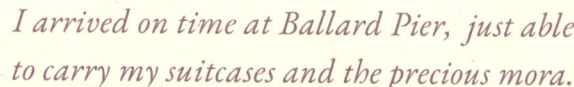

I arrived on time at Ballard Pier, just able
to carry my suitcases and the precious mora.

'What's that you've brought with you?' asked a smartly
uniformed steward as I mounted the gangway. 'Taking your
waste-paper basket along with you?' ... 'That's right,' I said.
'I'm a writer.'

BALLARD PIER

There's nothing I like better than a hot buttered toast, a freshly boiled egg and a dash of sweet mango chutney; this is usually my breakfast, and it sets me up nicely for the rest of the day.

Well, I had just peeled my egg and was busy buttering my toast, when I realized that I wasn't alone at the dining table. A glossy black jungle crow was sitting near the salt cellar, watching me with beady eyes. And before I could say good morning he seized my peeled egg and flew off through the open window.

I no longer have that crow sharing my breakfast.
But sometimes I miss the old fellow.

Being of a philosophical nature ... I got up,
closed the window, called the crow a crow,
and boiled myself another egg.

This was typical of those early days at Maplewood,
the cottage I'd rented on the outskirts of Mussoorie.
It was tucked away in a shelf of the hill.

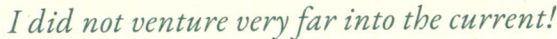

I did not venture very far into the current!

Rishikesh was then a small hamlet, with a few scattered ashrams. The river was pure and unpolluted.

*The most popular cinema hall
was the Picture Palace,*

which had opened in 1912, when
electricity had come to Mussoorie—
its original name was the Electric
Picture Palace

Fade in, fade out . . .
Another day, another picnic.

There are some people who, because of their personality or circumstances, stand out in this writer's memory more vividly than those who seemed more important in many ways.

Miss Kellner must have been in her sixties when I first saw her ... She seldom smiled, and I never heard her laugh, and I don't think she was particularly fond of small boys ... 'Do you know any card games?' she asked, and when I shook my head, she said, 'I'll teach you some easy ones.' And producing a pack of well-worn cards she taught me a simple but lively game called 'Snap'.

Miss Kellner was a heavily built woman with Nordic features ... had her own little hand-pulled carriage, and a pretty sight it was.

My first encounter with loneliness happened when I was seven, deposited by my mother in a convent boarding-school.

Was this what life was all about, being wrenched away from all that was homely and familiar, no matter how unhappy the home? I was miserable for days, hardly touching my food.

My walks, my books, the cinema, all helped me to be content with my own company. Sometimes I made a friend, but perhaps I was too intense, too demanding of friendship.

It took me some time before I learnt not to be too possessive. Late in 1951, when I was seventeen, I made that journey to England ... At first I went to Jersey, in the Channel Islands. I was very lonely there. It was a beautiful island ...

*I worked at several jobs, saved
some money, took off for London.*

... Lonely evenings at my typewriter,
conjuring up the India I'd left behind.

*Here we settled down under a whispering
pine and enjoyed our repast.*

And what did I like about London?

The theatres and the specialist cinemas—the Everyman in Hampstead, where I saw old films, and the Academy in Leicester Square, where I saw French and continental films. And Foyles Bookshop, where I could browse and pick up unusual books. But none of this was home.

*When I was a child in Jamnagar we had a wind-up
gramophone, and among the 78-rpm records that I used
to play, there was one called the 'The Lambeth Walk'*

... And so, on my explorations, I went down Lambeth Way, taking
the underground to Elephant and Castle and then walking around
Lambeth in search of musical Cockneys. But my only memorable
encounter was with a group of Teddy boys.

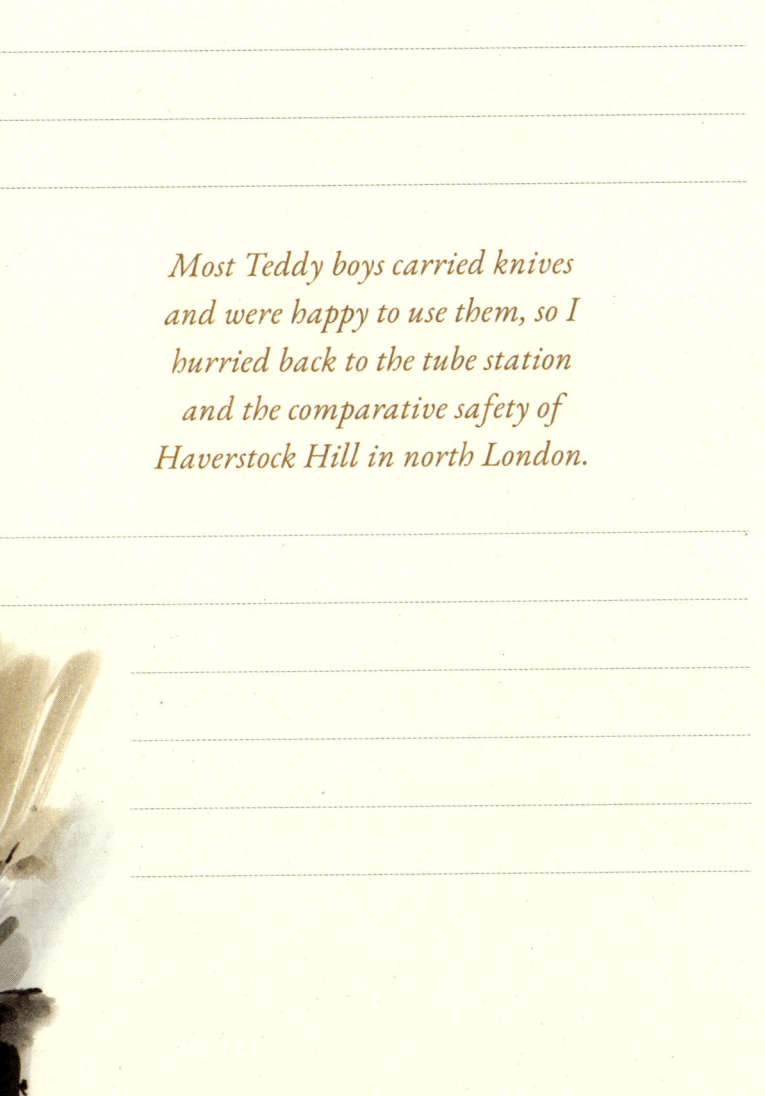

*Most Teddy boys carried knives
and were happy to use them, so I
hurried back to the tube station
and the comparative safety of
Haverstock Hill in north London.*

*In the summer of 1963, when
I came to live in Mussoorie ...*

> *'Some call it laziness . . .*
> *I call it deep thought.'*

I think it was Garfield the cat who said
that. Anyway, here I am in New Delhi,
circa 1960, searching for inspiration. I
had to move to the hills to find it.

I am not a powerful man,
just a frail human
full of faults and foibles;

but sitting on that knoll, in the
fragrance of the pine, and looking out
over the receding hills and the valley
beyond, I was filled with a sense of
well-being, of belief in myself.

We come into this world pure and innocent,

but it doesn't take long for us to be tainted and
corrupted by the warped civilization that prevails
around us—a world controlled by megalomaniacs,
fanatics, power-hungry individuals and self-
appointed guardians of our morals.

I grew up during the Nehru years.

He had no rivals. ... Nehru took his own
writing seriously but without pretension.
... Nehru understood the literary mind.

*Not many Englishmen settled on the land
or took to farming, unlike the colonials in
South Africa or Rhodesia ...*

But when Independence came, they had nowhere
to go—no friends, no family or relatives abroad,
and practically no income. Their savings soon dried
up. The garden became a wilderness. They fell
sick and couldn't get about. The tradesmen—the
boxwallahs—stopped coming. No bread, no milk.

And by home I meant India—its mud, its grass, its mango blossoms ... sugarcane juice, the boys on their bullock carts, the girls with jasmine-scented hair, the burning sunshine, cool water from an earthen surahi, the sharp tang of jamuns, the approach of heavily burdened monsoon clouds, palm trees waving, peepul leaves dancing, the banyan coming to life.

At my bedroom window in Landour. It's a windy spot and I have to keep the windows closed most of the time.

Sometimes the monkeys get in and I have a hard time evicting them; they make troublesome tenants. But I have a great view of the mountains and the valley.

Coming home from boarding school when I was ten, I found myself sharing the same bedroom as my sister, small brother and even smaller stepbrother, and after a few days of sulking I demanded (and got) a room of my own, albeit a tiny one, just an enclosed corner of the veranda.

It had a bed, a small table and a cane mora, or stool, and that was enough for me. I had flung my clothes into a cupboard in the children's room, and my school trunk was free to accommodate books, comics, a stamp album, an album of crests, another set of postcards (sent to me by my father, now gone), a cricket ball, a cup I'd won in an obstacle race (the only kind of race in which I excelled), a pocket knife, a walnut-wood stick (picked up in Simla) and a model airplane.

Destiny, or the Great Librarian,
brought me to this hilltop;
Mother Hill near Mother Ganga,
and here I have spent my best days
and done my best work. And
here I stay, until I have written
my last word.

Ruskin Bond's first novel, *The Room on the Roof*, written when he was seventeen, received the John Llewellyn Rhys Memorial Prize in 1957. Since then he has written a number of novellas (including *Vagrants in the Valley*, *A Flight of Pigeons* and *Mr Oliver's Diary*), essays, poems and children's books, many of which have been published by Penguin Books. He has also written over 500 short stories and articles that have appeared in magazines and anthologies.

He received the Sahitya Akademi Award in 1992, the Padma Shri in 1999 and the Padma Bhushan in 2014.

Ruskin was born in Kasauli, Himachal Pradesh, and grew up in Jamnagar, Dehradun, New Delhi and Simla. As a young man, he spent four years in the Channel Islands and London. He returned to India in 1955. He now lives in Landour, Mussoorie, with his adopted family.

Dan Williams lives and works in London.
Since graduating from the Royal College of Art in 1989
he has worked with many distinguished clients in the
publishing world.

In 2018 Dan illustrated a short prose poem by Khaled
Hosseini entitled *Sea Prayer*. An emotional response to
the current refugee crisis, it has since gone on to
receive international acclaim.